Poetry

2005

by
6th grade students of
Fairfield Middle School

"Where the Best Stuff is in the Middle"

1st WORLD LIBRARY
Literary Society

Poetry 2005

by 6th grade students of Fairfield Middle School

© 1st World Library - Literary Society, 2005
1100 North 4th St. Suite 131, Fairfield, Iowa 52556
• Tel: 641-209-5000 • Fax: 641-209-3001
• Web: www.1stworldlibrary.org

First Edition

LCCN: 2005908254

SoftCover ISBN: 1-59540-962-9
HardCover ISBN: 1-59540-968-8
eBook ISBN: 1-59540- 963-7

Foreword

Communication is vital in today's society. It comes in many forms these days, from conversing to e-mail. One form of communication is writing, and one form of writing is poetry. Poetry doesn't seem to get the recognition it deserves in this fast-paced world. It is a form of writing that is personal and demands time to read it. It needs to be understood or felt by the reader. It can represent self-exploration for the author, while it can open feelings in the reader. The poem becomes the symbol of communication on many levels to many people. We hope these poems will communicate to the readers in some meaningful way, as they are read.

This collection of poetry was created by the 6th grade students of Fairfield Middle School. It got started when a fifth grade student brought his poem home to his mother to read. His poem had been published in a book like this one. His mother is one of our sixth grade Language Arts/ Reading teachers. She saw it as an exciting project for the sixth graders at FMS. The rest is, as they say... history.

This book of poetry communicates to all that take the time to read it. Those who contributed their work hope you will let their poems communicate to you.

The collection of poems in this book started by sharing, and we hope you will share it with others, as you enjoy it yourself.

Gary Henry,
FMS Principal

Introduction

I am thrilled for my students to have this exciting opportunity to share their poetry with the world! In our poetry unit this year, our sixth graders read and memorized famous poems, were exposed to many different types of poetry, and tried their hand at writing their own poetry. Some of those poems include tanka, cinquain, haiku, acrostic, bio, concrete, diamante, ocean research, couplets, title down, and limericks. My students had fun creating poems that expressed who they really are. They also quickly discovered that writing poetry is very revealing, which can be scary. I am proud of their willingness to share this part of themselves with others. The openness and ease with which they write, along with their wit and honesty, simply amazes me. I hope you enjoy reading their work as much as I have. They should be very proud of their accomplishments.

Ann Gookin,
6th Grade Language Arts Teacher

I Will Never Ever Clean My Room
Inspired by my mom

I will never ever clean my room,
I don't care if it smells like a dead person's tomb!
There is nothing you can do to make me,
You can kick, bite, cry, and plea.
I won't fall for candies and sweets,
Not even for the most delightful treats.
You can torture me and put me in chains,
I can endure the most severe pains.
So as you can see, there is nothing you can do.
You might as well give up,
Even though my room smells like a zoo.
Allowance you say?
Two dollars is enough,
I'll do it for that pay!

Allissa Buelow
Age 12

Beautiful Sun

Sun rise, sun setting
Beautiful in the distance
A great thing to see
Sun rising early today
The sun setting late tonight.

Lani Eversage
Age 12

Lavender

Lavender is irises and lilacs and cat's fur.
Lavender is the taste of apple cider.
A hug makes me feel lavender.
Lavender is the sound of a whisper and a mother's voice.
Lavender is a garden, a comfy room, and a cabin in the mountains.
Looking at a baby is lavender.
Lavender is coming home.

Natasha Gorski
Age 12

Limerick

One day I was dining in France
A guy walked by with a glance
    He whistled at me
    I had so much glee
Then I decided I had no chance.

Samantha Byrnes
Age 12

Winter

Wonderland of white snow
Inches, even feet of it
Never want to go inside, unless for more clothes
Tactical maneuvers on the white battlefield
Evade the flying balls of ice and snow
Retreat! Back to the house!

Jacob Lantz
Age 12

Sailor

I am a sailor, a daughter of the sea.
I'm a sea otter, and I'm swimming free.
Haha, I'm as happy as can be!
Right now I'm swimming past your boat.
I never struggle to stay afloat.
Eating fish, crabs, mollusk, and clams.
I'm living a good life…living it grand.
I'm a very funny creature with small ears, and a great
whopping tail.
I'm out in the ocean, ready to sail!
My fur keeps me warm, even in the coldest weather.
Chasing two fish, and catching them together!
I'm swimming fast now, to catch up with my friends.
Swaying my whole body to catch up with them.
I'm going quite fast and I chortle as I go past.
Now I'm looking up at a big, beautiful sky
Thinking this is a good time to be alive.
I love to sail and I will always do so.
Watch me swim past your boat…watch me go.

Bethany Larson
Age 12

Haiku

Snowflake memories
Dropping on my cold wet tongue
Loving the winter.

Kayla Ledger
Age 12

Racing

Riding around the track slowly,
And then the flag goes green.
Cars start flying around the track.
In the stands are the fans.
"Number 40 takes the lead," says the announcer.
Go, go, go!

Dakota Simmons
Age 12

What Is Green?

Green is emeralds and grass and feels slippery or slimy.

Green is the taste of Granny Smith apples.

A hilly roller coaster makes me feel green.

Green is the sound of trees blowing and frogs croaking.

Green is summer gardens, green houses, and the bottom of a pond.

Running in a meadow is green.

Green is a spring day.

Nikia Story
Age 12

A Fool

There once was a fool,
And he fell into a pool
    Not once but twice
    And he has lice
And his coat was made from wool.

Shyanna Smith
Age 12

Best Friends

I have a friend, she is the best,
We do everything together,
And after that we rest.
We swim in the dim,
We shop 'til we drop.
But now she isn't the best.
We don't do everything together,
Nor do we rest.
We don't swim in the dim,
Nor shop 'til we drop.
I miss her.
Hopefully she will come back,
But not now,
Not next month or week.
Maybe in a year,
I hope, man, was she dear.
And I loved her to tears,
All the years
We spent together,
I hope she still remembers me.
Someday, maybe she will come and
We can have some tea.

But I will remember her,
I will never forget
She was my best friend that I will never
Regret.

Abby Stickels
Age 12

The Horse of the Gulf

I'm the wonderful Lined Seahorse.
I'm a poor swimmer and depend on camouflage to hide from my enemies.
I come in many colors like light brown, dusky gray, brick red, and orange.
I have a toothless mouth.
I have a tubular snout.
I don't have a spine.
I have a dorsal fin.
I eat eel grass and sar grass.
You can find me in the Gulf of Mexico.
My size is five inches.
My other name is Hippocanpus Guttulatus.
I scrutinize everything I see.
I'm the smallest of seahorses.

Michael Smith
Age 12

Color

Red is blood and roses and hot.
Red is the taste of atomic fireballs.
Being embarrassed makes me feel red.
Red is the sound of a siren and yelling.
Red is Hell, a fire station, and stuff in your body.
Sunburn is red.
Red is painful.

Travis Schombert
Age 12

Limerick

There once was a boy named Ted,
Who fell and broke his head.
　　He fell on the ice
　　It wasn't that nice.
Now he is staying in bed.

Devon Ryan
Age 12

Title Down

Shining in the dark night sky
They are sometimes being looked at night time
Always in the sky looking oh, so bright
Red, they never are. They are always gold and yellow.

Samantha Ruckman
Age 12

The Pasture

By Robert Frost and Me

I'm going out to play basketball;
When I go to shoot,
I hope I make a hoop.
I shan't be gone long- - - You come tool

I'm going out to talk on my cell;
To chat with a friend,
Hoping the day won't end.
I shan't be gone long - - - You come too.

**Kassie Myers
Age 12**

Couplets

I fell down the stairs
And lost all my hair.

I was running down the street
Tripping on my clumsy feet.

I fell on a tack
And broke my back.

I ran into a wall
And had a big fall.

I lost my shoe,
Now what do I do?

Jordan Leazer
Age 12

Black

Black cats
Long and fast
And mean.
Cats are
Kooky.

Zach Petersburg
Age 12

The Harp Of The Sea

I am the Harp Seal, kind and furry,
I swim to the ocean floor in a hurry.
I grow about as long as two meters,
My family and I are all big eaters.
Arctic cod and capelin are my favorite treat,
Although there are other things that I like to eat.
I am pretty big, about five hundred pounds,
I can bark, wail, and make other sounds.
My pup blends in with the snow 'cause it is white,
I like to dive around and swim at night.
I live up by the North Pole, that is true,
So you won't find me in Timbuktu.
I got to go, so see you later,
Oh, and watch out for the Sea Alligator.

Brian Jennings
Age 12

Cheerleading

Cheerful girls
Help support the team
Excited
Energetic
Ready
Loud. They
Even match with their outfits.
A dance is sometimes
Done during half-time
In the center of the field.
Now the game is over
Goodbye to the night and ready for the next game.

Chelsea Parker
Age 12

Blue

Blue is jeans and shirts and soft.
Blue is the taste of blueberries.
Babies crying make me feel blue.
Blue is houses, the ocean, and stores.
Not doing anything is blue.
Blue is slow songs, and not being with you.

Sidney Lowe
Age 13

Limerick

There was a baker who was thin.
He won a big metal bin.
    He went home to cook
    And he took a look
At the big metal bin again.

Matt Hotek
Age 12

The Pasture

By Robert Frost and Me

I'm going out to go to Hawaii:
I'm stepping on the smooth white sand
Hopefully when I come back, I will be tanned,
I shan't be gone long. — You come too.

**Lauren Holt
Age 12**

My Eight Feet

My colors vary from gray to blue,
Maybe even a color close to you.
When I get mad or scared I squirt out ink,
It smells like me, so it must stink.
If you come near me I will use my jet,
I do this because I'm not here to pet.
You can find me in the ocean where it's warm,
I have a beak so I will warn.
I eat lobsters and crabs and even more,
I glide along the ocean floor.
My scientific name if Octopus Vulgaris, isn't it neat?
I wonder if it has anything to do with my eight feet?

Shelby Mauck
Age 11

Limerick

There once was a guy from Spain
Who thought he could jump out of a plane
    He forgot his chute
    While putting on his boot
And right now he's in pain.

Brandyn Martin
Age 12

Summer (Tanka)

Wonderful summer,
I wrote about it before,
But I love it so,
I shall write about it more,
And I will always love it.

Paris Chookolingo
Age 11

The Smooth Sun Star of the North

I am the Smooth Sun Star
     of the Arctic to Cape Cod
          and Alaska to Puget Sound.
On the rock and gravel bottoms
     I crawl.
Small sea cucumbers
     and other small sea stars
          are what I eat.
My seven to fourteen arms
     make me
          one of two
               many-armed
                    starfish in
                        Great Britain.

I'm usually
     purplish or red
     pink or orange
     with a pale underside.
I am sixteen inches wide
     with a rough surface.
I don't have to be a baby

because I directly become an egg
to an adult.
I am the Smooth Sun Star
with the tips of my arms
usually turned up.

Edna Jones
Age 12

Green Is

Green is grass and bushes and lots of money.
Green is the taste of apples.
Being outdoors makes me feel green.
Green is the sound of eating celery and waving money.
Green is in a tree, in a meadow, in a yard.
Lying in our yard in spring is green.
Green is cool air.

Ben Hendershot
Age 12

The Pasture

I'm going out to ride the four-wheeler:
I'll only stop to take a break
But I'll be back to bake a cake
I shan't be gone long — you come too.

Nichole Bruegge & Robert Frost
Age 12

Purple—A Color Poem

Purple is Barney & bruises & bumpy.
Purple is the taste of plums.
Holding your breath makes me feel purple.
Purple is the sound of the pop of gum & the squish
of plums.
Purple is the sky, the sunset, & a candy store.
Eating grapes is purple.
Purple is bruised like Tom Cruise.

Tyler Hausner
Age 12

This Is For My Sake

I stay home so I could bake a cake.
When I'm done, I try to awake so I can make a steak.
I go to the door, "Hey, there's Drake!"
We take a handshake while I watch a snake shake.
I see a snowflake when I awake.
I listen to the news and hear there will be an earth-
quake.
I say, "For Pete's sake, please give me a break!"
NOW I'm awake.

Liz Heilmann
Age 12

Love

I love you, but you love her.
I could have saved
all the tears you made me cry
to drown you in them. Why did
I fall for you?
You make me feel invisible.
Yesterday you smiled
at me. For the
whole ten seconds
I thought the sun had come
out. I love you with
all my heart. I love
you, but you don't even know me.
You're with that girl again. If
I was that pretty would
you like me?
Why do guys fall for girls like that?
Here you come walking down the hallway.
Your hair is flowing in the wind.
I love you so much it turns to hate.

Taylor Eaton
Age 12

Blade–A Title Down Poem

Bloody with fear
Leathered in metal
Attacks everyone in his way
Death is upon those with bloody fangs and
Extreme forces become unleashed

Josh Harrison
Age 12

Dugong

I am a Dugong, chubby as can be,
I live near Australia in the deep blue sea.
I can't go too far from the shore,
But as I swim, I can carry my baby upon my back.
All I eat is seaweed and grass,
It's kinda like a diet, but I still get fat.
I am related to the manatee and the elephant, too,
Even though he is on land and I am in the sea.
I have rough gray skin and tusks that grow,
But the girls usually don't get tusks, unless they're old.
I use streamline strokes and am so graceful,
But was once mistaken for a mermaid.

Dana Diers
Age 11

Skateboarding

Sunny days is when I do it
Knowing that I'll fall
All the time. I scrape my knees
Trying to let them heal.
Everyone is watching me
Bothering me when I skate.
Other people encourage me
All the others just hate.
Reading a list to see if I won
Don't get mad if I don't.
I'll keep trying
Never quit and never
Give up hope.

Orlando Ferguson
Age 12

Weird Town

There once was a lady from Jatt
Whose arms were made like a cat's
    She scratched pretty hard
    But she had a bad guard
So then she got hit with a bat.

Taylor Johnston
Age 11

The Pasture

By Robert Frost and Me

I'm going out to ride the four-wheeler:
I'll go over big jumps
And land with big thumps:
I shan't be gone long—You come too.

I'm going out to play some baseball:
I'll try to hit a home run
And it will be a lot of fun
I shan't be gone long—You come too.

Brock Haines
Age 12

Title Down

Bat
A home run
Strike three
Eight to eight
Bye, bye ball, home run
A win
Lost out in the field
Lost over the fence

**Jordan Van Blaricom
Age 12**

Limerick

There once was a boy from Nantucket
Who stuck his foot in a bucket
   "My foot really hurts bad
   It was broken by you, lad,"
He said to his friend, Tucket.

**Sebastian Sheehan
Age 11**

Diamante

War
Bloody, chaos
Killing, dying, shooting
Destruction, enemies, calm, happy
Cheering, hugging, laughing
Happy, joyful
Peace

Ricky Stewart
Age 13

5 Couplets

1. Don't show-off to get a dog
    'Cause you might lose it in the bog.

2. I got a fish
    How come you got a dish?

3. Social studies is my favorite class
    I hope today we catch a big bass!

4. My friend's name is Tanna
    She really likes bananas.

5. Tanna's brother's name is Cody
    Sometimes he gets really grody!

**Veronica Payne,
Age 12**

Pink

Pink is bubble gum and my shoes and is soft.
Pink is the taste of strawberries.
After I get my hair done makes me feel pink.
Pink is the sound of baby laughter and puppies
barking.
Pink is a mansion, an ice cream shop, and a baby
girl's room.
Pink is relaxing.
Pink is ME!

Rachel Morgan
Age 12

Outside

Swaying in the wind
Ever so very happy
Trunks start swaying merrily
Cause today we go to play

Dylan McClure
Age 11

Couplets

I cast to the right
And I got a bite.

I was starting a race
I got a good pace.

I went to ride my bike
It's something I really like.

I went to school
Even though I wanted to go to the pool.

You are way too tall
You can barely walk in the hall.

Dalton Laux
Age 12

Diamante

IRAQ
Scary, frightening
Fighting, shooting, dying
Dangerous, small, big, safe
Willing, preparing, freeing
Strong, brave
AMERICA

Bryan Kephart
Age 12

Limerick

I once "borrowed" my sister's shoes
I broke them and cried the blues.
    Now I will ask before I take
    For my sister's yelling sake.
Oh yeah, and I got a big bruise.

Olivia Hunt
Age 12

Pink

Pink is blood and people and the summer night sky.
Pink is the taste of fried eggs.
My skin makes me feel pink.
Pink is the sound of pigs and strawberries.
Pink is flowers, pizza, and tasty fruit.
In the morning the sun is pink.
Pink is a town or restaurant.

**Darren Cassiday
6th Grade**

The Pasture

I am going out to play ball:
I'll bat, hit, and sweat,
I don't think I will get wet
I shan't be gone long—you come too.

**Shelby Davisson and Robert Frost
Age 12**

Newspaper

I went to the newspaper and bought an ad
It was on how to subtract and add
    I am afraid
    That it might fade
But it was really quite bad.

Ashley Fields
Age 12

Ten Parrots—A Limerick

If you know Miss Trolley Lolley
You'd know she had ten parrots named Polley.
    They all went to heaven
    Not all, but just seven.
The rest, they all suffered in Holley.

**Lizzie Hamilton
Age 11**

Saxaphone

Awesome saxaphone
Plays a jazzy tune for you
The best instrument.

**Danielle Hannes
Age 12**

Bob Rob

There is a dog whose name is Bob
He really, really likes to rob
    He entered a house
    And then met a mouse
Who said, "Time to finish the job!"

Ramses Alonso
Age 12

Cleaner of the Ocean Reefs

I'm a Cleaner Shrimp.
My scientific name is steno pus hispidus.
Wow, that's really hard to say.
If you're a fish and you want cleaned, you can find me in the coral reefs.
If you're one who doesn't like bacteria, well they're food to me, so come get cleaned.
If you hold still, I will clean you, but you must be patient because there will be a line.
But if you take me out of the water, fish will keep coming back for a week and I will be gone.
I get all the warm weather because I'm mostly tropical and I have five pair of walking legs.
I must be a risk-taker because I clean more eels than cleaner fish do.
I have a big job for such a small shrimp, for I'm only two inches high.
I'm the Cleaner Shrimp.

Nykole Thacker
Age 12

Rachel

Funny, short, smart, athletic
Sister of Keri, April, Mike, Daniel
Lover of sports, reading, animals
Who feels good everyday, stressed after school, tired at night
Who needs good grades, skinny waist, pimple-free face
Who gives friends 100%, love, hope
Who fears the dark, scary people, detention
Who would like to see Hawaii, Germany, Ireland
Resident of Fairfield; Libertyville Road
SCHWARZ

**Rachel Schwarz
Age 12**

Friend

Forever we will be
Running
Indeed you and me
Enjoying the time together
Nothing can put us
Down, for together we stand

Emma Ryan
Age 12

Limerick

There once was a cat named Jake
Who wanted to learn how to bake
    Curiosity killed the cat
    But I think it was a bat
So he never got to bake a cake.

**Travis Heckethorn
Age 12**

Clown'n Around

I am a clown fish!
That is white and orange!
2-5 inches is my length!
Very strong is my strength!

I live on the ocean floor,
And I don't have a door!
I live in an anemone!

I eat plankton and some fish
But not any pufferfish!

I lay my eggs under an anemone!
The tentacles don't even sting me!!

I clean my fellow anemone's wastes!
Good thing I don't have very good taste!

I also scare away his enemies!
Because they are very scared of me!

I am a clown fish!
That is white and orange!!

Haliegh Hanshaw
Age 12

Diamante

Cats
Furry, smooth,
Meowing, purring, playing,
Calico, feline, Chihuahua, angel,
Barking, growling, rolling
Smelly, rough,
Dogs

Sami Fisher
Age 12

Limerick

Once I had a dog
Who hung around with a cat in a log
    I like that cat
      Because it's wearing a hat
But I lost that cat in a fog.

Brittany Craff
Age 12

Diamante

Fire
Light, Hot
Burning, Heating, Lighting
Firemen, Firetruck, Vapor, Liquid
Cooling, Freezing, Boiling
Blue, Cool
Water

Ethan Cox
Age 12

Haiku

Sunrise and sunset
Beautiful are both of them,
Each day and each night

Ashley Atwood
Age 11

Limerick

I once had a dog
Who hung out in a log
    But, of course, all fat toads
    Leave big loads
So he never hung out in a bog.

Rachel Swanson
Age 12

Word Cinquain

Mitzy
Black Schnauzer
She is calm
She is very sweet
German

**Stephanie Adam
Age 11**

Write Your Own Poem

Write Your Own Poem

Write Your Own Poem

Write Your Own Poem

Write Your Own Poem

Write Your Own Poem

Write Your Own Poem

Write Your Own Poem

Write Your Own Poem

Write Your Own Poem

Write Your Own Poem

Write Your Own Poem

Write Your Own Poem

Write Your Own Poem

Write Your Own Poem

Write Your Own Poem

Write Your Own Poem

Write Your Own Poem

Write Your Own Poem

Write Your Own Poem

Write Your Own Poem

Write Your Own Poem

Write Your Own Poem

Write Your Own Poem

Write Your Own Poem

Write Your Own Poem

Write Your Own Poem

Write Your Own Poem

Write Your Own Poem

www.ingramcontent.com/pod-product-compliance
Lightning Source LLC
LaVergne TN
LVHW011408080426
835511LV00005B/433